CHARITY
BEGINS AT HOME

By June Dutton
Illustrated by Susan Perl

FAITH □ HOPE □ CHARITY
(Three Little Books in a Box)
Charity Begins at Home
Text © 1981 Determined Productions, Inc.
Illustrations © 1981 Susan Perl
World Rights Reserved
ISBN: 0-915696-46-0
Library of Congress Catalog Card Number: 80-69798
Printed in Singapore

Charity is leaving
the last cookie
for someone else
when you want it
more than anything
yourself.

Charity is
laughing at your
friend's jokes
even when
they're not
funny.

Charity is
not making a face
when someone steps
on your toes.

Charity is letting your friend ride your new bike even when you don't want him to.

Charity is spending the last of your allowance on someone else.

Charity is
watching
someone else's
favorite TV show
rather than
your own.

Charity is
listening
when you'd rather
be talking.

Charity is helping with someone else's homework after you've finished your own.

Charity is
taking time
to explain things
to people who will
never understand
anyway.

Charity is
what parents...

**need lots
and lots of.**

Charity is
admitting
you're wrong
even when no one
asks you to.

Charity is
managing to smile
when you'd
rather frown...
or maybe
even cry.

Charity is saving a place in the front row for someone who's always late.

Charity is
pretending
to be interested
when you're not.

Charity is
giving in
when you
don't really
need to.